MISTAKEN FOR SONG

— WINNER OF THE 2008 LEXI RUDNITSKY POETRY PRIZE —

MISTAKEN FOR SONG

POEMS | TARA BRAY

A KAREN & MICHAEL BRAZILLER BOOK
PERSEA BOOKS/NEW YORK

Copyright © 2009 by Tara Bray.

Persea Books, Inc.
853 Broadway
New York, NY 10003

Printed in the U.S.A.
Designed by Bookrest.
First edition.

Library of Congress Cataloging-in-Publication Data

Bray, Tara, 1965-
Mistaken for song : poems / Tara Bray. — 1st ed.
p. cm.

"A Karen & Michael Braziller book."
ISBN 978-0-89255-347-1 (original trade pbk. : alk. paper)
I. Title.

PS3602.R397M57 2009
811'.6—dc22

2008037956

for Bill

Contents

ONE.

Carolina Chickadees

Another moment struck by the shenanigans
of the chickadees, their songs, pert shavings
of glee, the dart of their tight round bodies
dressed in a clean contrast: black on white,
little skunk joys, little wingbeat-whippets
my palm hungers for, instinctively.
Pulses pinging from trees to the feeder,
back and again, until the spare appetite
we assigned to their tiny beaks
seems another sham believed into simile.
They whip and dip, sled quick slopes
of air, and I plead to feel them beat
upon my ear, chatter, tease me,
meek cheek-fires I want to swallow whole.

The Wolf

We drove Mt. Comfort Road at dusk, turned right
on dirt, my daily walking ground. Two cats
fought there, clawed each other while we grew tense
inside their screams. Think of filth, dust
and burrs, their open wounds, spitty hisses,
needle teeth. I rolled the window up.
The sky was gray on gray. I dragged her out
to see if what was dead and sprawling
down the bank—its foot caught in barbed wire—
was what I thought it was: a wolf,
its fur the gray of rainless dirt
and silky-clean as nothing tame can be.

Hesitant, we got out of the car.
I watched the fear come down on her.
Look, I needed something I couldn't face alone.
She pointed a flashlight at the animal.
It's just a dog, she said, the face, the size.
The ride home was quiet.

That was weeks ago.
It's still there, stinking up the road,
smaller now. Every time
I pass, I stare. It's fallen down the bank.
The birds have eaten a hole of blackness
through the skin, cleaned out the gut,
and soon the jawbone will show through
until bone and a dusting of fur will be all that's left;
then not even that. I believe something wilder
than a dog is there. I try to say a prayer
each time I pass, and usually don't forget.

The Preparation

Go to the woman whose mother died young.
She can tell you the downfall
of self sufficiency. Take your worst day,
move everything under it. Your heavens
will be gray with the smog of toil,
or if it's her determined jaw you want, take
the file, begin edging off your own bone,
your arms growing hard, angled, your eyes
setting themselves deeply for the kill.
This is the preparation. It is not like the hunter
dousing his skin with urine, nor the thief
pulling the black shirt over his body.
You need not pack provisions, nor send up prayers
while you offer yourself
broken and whispering a beggar's song.
I tell you nothing prepares you
for a mother crumpled on cold tile, gone
in seconds on a night you were not home.
Imagine yourself untended
as the garden behind the empty house.
Your clothing will grow small,
tattered, and no one will notice.
This is the stumbling into loneliness,
a girl's knees tearing open,
this child you will cling to with tired fingers.
How you will hate to pull the woman's voice
from your throat. You'd rather scrub scum
from the bathroom floor, barehanded, without water.
Do you feel what I tell you in the dust
you are breathing? You will.
It will be everything you never asked for.

Up in the Cottonwood

The kestrel trapped a sparrow in its claws,
pressing past its captive to the branch beneath.
The smaller bird went limp,
then thrust itself into a fluttering protest,
then went limp again, back and forth,

the kestrel calm, so lean-eyed.
Ease is what I saw, and grace.
The sparrow, revealing not one slit of beauty,
was only body—clamp, struggle, dampness—
fighting for this world, beneath two claws

that pierced its softness like a rhapsody,
the kestrel fully alive in order to create a little dying.
Two birds caught up
in what some might step back from
or count themselves in luck to see.

They loomed above, spilling down reality
like elders chock full of elegance and grit.
There is a glimmer to disaster, a calm stone
at survival's core. So natural, those darklings,
all around them sky and green.

Once

I climbed the bale of hay to watch the heron
in the pond. He waded a few steps out,
then back, thrusting his beak under water,
pulling it up empty. Later I walked the roads
for miles, certain he'd be there when I returned.
How is it for him, day after day, brittle legs rising
from warm green scum, his graceful neck curled,
damp in the bright heat? It's a dull world.
Every day, the same roads, the sky,
the dust, the barn caving into itself,
the tin roof twisted and scattered in the yard.
Again, the bank covered with oxeye daisy
that turns to spiderwort, to chicory,
and at last to goldenrod. Each year, the birds—
thick in the air and darting in wild numbers—
grow quiet, the grasses thin, the light leaves
earlier each day. The heron stood
stone-still on the bale when I returned.
And then, his wings burst open, lifting
the steel-blue rhythm of his body into flight.
I touched the warm hay, hoping for a trace
of his wild smell, then cupped my hands over
my face—nothing but the heat of fields and skin.
It wasn't long before the world
began to breathe the beat of ordinary hours,
stretching out again beneath the sky.

Rainstorm

I want to throw my body into rain
and run for miles. I want
my hair slick-black against my skull,
the world drenched in a wet shine.
I take what I want with steady steps.

The dogs run out,
wired from the approaching storm.
Their fur is weighted down with rain,
mud and stink, their mouths thick with rage.
I stop and walk, cooing to get them calm.
Most I win over—the foolish ones.
For those that hate me to the end,
I feel camaraderie, despite the threat
of their quick teeth. They hold back.
I keep moving on,

wanting to hear the branches crack like bones
then crash to earth, to feel the sting of rain
against my fists, these pale wet stones
out in another storm. I want the trees
to shake me back to all I've lost,
to warn, then shed pieces of their lives.
I'm exhaling the time away; it's late.
I call the storm out loud,
more alive and breathing harder as I go.

I was not a girl who dreamed of horses and a barn,
but when I run upon a horse who's come
to the field's edge to rub her neck

against barbed wire that drips with rain,
I rush. Beneath the rumbling sky,
I search the brown grass for any shoots
of green, tug strands for her, feeling the way
grass can leave slits in the skin. We shiver
as the storm begins to break around us
onto the battered roads.

Breathing, breathing, the two of us—I rest
grass against her mouth; she's taking it in.
I'm talking, talking to her through the rain
that pours as something
thunders in my hands that reach and find
her warm, find her frightening
and real as her mouth, full of green.
The dogs are barking madly a mile away.

In a stab of light my body knows how it feels
to press barbed wire into your skin, to rub
yourself until you blur into the dusk,
to forget the night that falls fast
before you find the way back home.
I want to throw this body into rain
and soak it up, drop by drop. I want
to be the darkest animal that sucks it in
and roams out in the storm before she sleeps.

Perfect

I loved those early mornings
when I slipped into the untouched
pool to skim the bottom,
dark arrow gliding inside the stillness.
I loved the late afternoons,
learning to execute perfect
jackknives, pikes,
layouts from the diving board.
And he was there
when I rose from the water,
the bronze, familiar body,
the wet black hair,
my father calling out
The feet fell apart on entry, or
the splash too large, or tuck
tighter to increase the rate of spin,
each word a blessing. His voice
held the power to shape movement.
Straight and tall, he stood alone
to watch a girl working like mad
to be perfect, the sun beating down.
I was happy. This was how
I learned water.
There were no diving teams
in Donalsonville, Georgia,
but there was my father delivering
scores, *Six, Four, Nine,*
the soft molding of a body returning
to water, a girl working herself
into glorious exhaustion.

The Back Walkover

The summer my mother died
a neighbor drove me to gymnastics.
Round-off, and I sailed skyward, backwards,
fetal position, spinning. The coach's hand
did not rest on my back. I still
feel his absent touch,
the shock of my feet hitting the mat,
as he yelled *Chin up. Suck it in.*
That a girl. My legs crumbled.

Today my students meet for tumbling club,
thrust airy bodies upward
knowing they will be carried.
The smallest girl with fearless eyes
works on her back walkover. She curls,
and I kneel, place my hand under her arch.
When she whirls her leg to the sky, I give
her calf a gentle push. Again and
again she makes it. Her leg. My hand.

I want to say the light comes in,
slants its golden arm
as an offering to this child and her teacher
in the center of the gym, but the room grows
dark, bitter. A heaviness is there.
I hold her with the tired arms
of a young girl who lifted herself
out of bed to the school bus
and back to that motherless home.

I want to drop the small gymnast,

pray for forgiveness as I let her slip
between the open spaces.

How My Mother Died

My father shook the gun to get the bullet out.
He was a careless man, but only once.
I shouldn't linger on this, the road rising out of itself,
my father out on Pine Street in the dark,
down on all fours, trying to open up his face
with gravel, trying to get down to the tar
of what went wrong by making blood again.
They find him there in a dream of twigs
thrashing in the heat, every stitch of light withheld.

Jesus of the ordinary prayer,
lay my father down on a bed of straw
and let him bleed his way to light.
Give him one sweet hour of oblivion,
for all of us. He's out there groveling
in the glare of suspicion, burrowing into the deep
red pit where the lowest sounds are made.
He's borrowed his life from brambles that wait to burn.
I know the dirt won't hide our family,
and the sun's intensity won't take root in the sky,
make truth a thing we all can see.
So let my father drift away from here
holding your brown feet.
Stir your crown of glory into his bleary eyes and sing
the untroubled prayer, the warm treason of innocence.
Ready us both for the undoing,
that can't, for the life of him, be undone.

Motherless

Brothers shedding funeral clothes,
with hands that smell of onion grass,

then sleeping on stained sheets
and pulsing like a creek bubbling with rain,

Brothers walking home with river feet,
Brothers at their sister's neck like sun,

Brothers of the fields picking thorns from legs,
small limbs sprinkled with faint ticks of blood,
Brothers hearing gunshots in the sky,

Brothers standing still to watch the blue jays
stab a cake of suet in a cage,
Blood boys alive as two peppers, ripe in the hand,

Brothers sinking when they are alone,
brooding in chairs of pine,
each seat a glossy mother-heart,

Brothers swimming in a ditch when things get bad,
stink on stink in the cool relief of mud froth,
the ruin of standing rain,

Brothers of the aftermath,
tussling under dirty southern trees,
Boys serving as disciples of the grass,

the soaked red dirt, the lovely violence
dreaming up the light of goldenrod at night,
Brothers blazing as they weep,
making mothers from women they half know,

Brothers singing songs
their father taught, songs of summer dust
and bean hulls rotting in a paper bag.

Touch

Call it grace, the smell of him, the smell of dirt.
Fifteen and we were lost in the ground's heat.
No street lights deep in those woods; I'd made sure.
Some things I wanted to save or hide. I let
his hand roam, but only in the dark.
Once, after we'd explored the flesh awhile
and calmed our rushing breath,
he said, "Let's pray to God and tell Him thanks.
So much He has fulfilled." Afraid, I knelt
and went along. Out loud, we voiced
our gratefulness for just how good it felt;
then off we ran as if we were being chased
by graven men with hands of greater sin
than we would ever know, or so I thought.
Sometimes our spirits racing at such a high,
we'd leap into the air and swat our hands
at the stars, playing like children younger
than we were, until we reached our bikes
tucked back in tall grass. He'd go his way;
I'd go mine after a high five.
I can still hear the sound of tires on pavement,
the rush of air making room for us to leave.
At home we'd find the will to wake at two a.m.
I'd call him. We'd talk of God
until the sun rose, in whispers soft and pure.
I found a thrill lurking in our late-night mumblings,
the first time I'd ever spoken to another of such things.
If there is a God, He loved us then, blessed
our bodies waking to earth and hunger, that much
I believe. But the van came anyway

and moved my family on to another town.
And he became a man of God, turned
from earthly things and me. Those fifteen years
have doubled now. Yet sometimes I still wake
at two a.m., turn on Loretta Lynn
or Emmylou so low I won't disturb
the neighbors beneath me. In whispers in the dark
I sing, soft and slow, lost in those songs
that burn my darkest places down.
I remember long ago, a doubting girl,
I learned to touch, and I was touched;
I woke at night and spoke of God;
for the first time, I tasted fire.

TWO.

Spiderwort After Storm

Imagine this: three purple
silken handkerchiefs
overlapped; stamen tips, six
drops of yellow blood
caught up in purple lint; three
buds trimmed in red the hue
of heat pulsing in a thumb;
each leaf, a green slow spiral
of a dancer's arm holding
out her gift, nothing more
than one pale breath of grass.

Snap the stem and find
slobber that spurs esteem,
not love. The petals lose
their way at dusk, unmake
themselves, turning it all
to a liquid porch of grief.
The hairy omen sways
in wind that chills; eyes—
sharp enough to prick—
ease in. The day is darkly
cold, and yet we live.

To My Mother's Death

Early riser, it is your sermon I hear, the thud of feet on pine,
the birdsong bargaining in a darkness not prepared to leave,

Earth-tender, breathing slowly over the land's sorrow,

And still I find ways to forget the bullet scar in the bathroom wall,
my mother's backbone ruined, that fractured hour,
the mirroring of a girl's cold hand,

And once, years ago I watched her lock her eyes on an old woman
leaving bread for crows at the corner of a parking lot,

This too impressed me—my mother's long legs folded into wings,
the smooth curves of slender river feet,

The tea-drop on her lip,

And all this,

The gun discharged and then. And yet. And.

On certain days in spite of it, I find myself pounding away
                                        at the pulpit of delight,

      coneflower
      coreopsis
      spring beauty
      bergamot

Early riser sleeping when cicadas sing,

Earth's redemption: melon, almond butter, coriander, orange zest
slope of his belly, smell of scalp and clean shirts

crow spread open like a glove

avocado doused in lemon juice

Wholesome titmouse, never plain, opening its eyes until the end—
bitter, worthy, tart with grace.

Prayer

May the purple taste of lament
dust our mouths of separation.

May the postures of old men and all
their quiet suffering join our arms.

May death's golden hill
break our bodies into one spark

of breath, one dance of form.
May we stand together, still

as earth's brown table, humble
trees in a blue-eyed field of chicory.

Departure in New Mexico

How I hated the grandeur of that sky
we rode fifteen-hundred miles to meet
at dusk with its sturdy pinks and golds,
the glimmer you beheld, the light
that in the heat of day beat its fire
against my hands and stung my chest.
You gave yourself over to its drunken heaven
of vastness, cocking back your head
to absorb the slow claim of sun, the God-burn,
the open rush—your voice rising like mist
into what would soon swallow you whole,

leaving me with the thin wind
of this soiled heart one more time.
That night I prayed to be good,
as if goodness might keep you,
and for the first time in years I ate meat,
relieved to hold that death on my tongue.
I wanted to devour something, taking flesh
into my cave of barking bones
and moon-bred hands before calling you home
one last time with a silky voice of reason.
Still you remained, and I returned to my sky,
small and pale, connecting to nothing
but the bitter taste of heart torn softly in its place.

Listen, it's been years. Your face has faded
into the haze, and still the Ozark sky
on a strangely bright day can jar me
enough to shut my blinds and long for leaves

that make damp shade out of despair,
for the lusty forest floor, the green relief above
allowing only dimes of light to touch my face
like a litany, like a picking clean,
like the crumbs of a shy girl's prayer.

For good,

I've shut my window to the sound of waking birds,
and every day I set out to meet a woman dying.
No more trinkets to give away—just praise for the girl
who licks quick crosses in the floor until her tongue bleeds.
She claims pain you make yourself is saintly in the hands
and doubles your beauty. Perhaps I'll steal again,
words or time. This world demands our breath, then blood,
that shy river of warmth, then each delicate bone.
Who wants to be strong? The woman will not speak of dying,
her brow a contraction, her sternum near petrified,
as if the body's truth is hardness. She is real, and still
I ignore the old tongue calling, *brother, sister*. Birdsong—
an absence I have built with my own hands.

Years, and still

I cannot say my mother's name
burned in the back of my throat,
fallen like that last petal,
shaped like a tear, or a tear,
as in—tear the petals one by one,
shred them, leave the pistil naked.
Pluck the stamens off like little sores.

Born Again

She prowls a land of too many cats
who flash their eyes, small beads of hate,
the dogs using their own filth to fight
each required loyalty, armadillos sleeping shattered
on roads that wind their skinny necks away.
Only the houses hurt, weeping from torn screens
that leak their stinks into the night.
All along, this is what she longed for,
the swallows to come slice away her grief,
the beetle broken in her hand, the coon that swaggers,
a place to bed down in the breezeless afternoon.

Sabbath

The day you left, the marsh grass stopped me cold.
I wanted to comb it, but really
I wanted my fingers to bleed.

It was the season I saw three pelicans
dip back their heads and let the fish fall to orange light.
Certainly they couldn't stand to swallow.
I knew the intensity of pulling in the throat, that pained rippling
of flesh forced down, and how it weighs and weighs.

When you left, I wanted to home in on just one bird,
know it the way I knew my own mouth's taste,
the taste that stays and stays. But the birds,
dozens, took me by surprise; so many unfamiliars,
a vibrato of wingspans and offbeat songs.
Come out of the margins, the songs cried. Flight is not enough.
I'd grown accustomed to being the dry distant thing
who wanted to sneak up on the real,
to fabricate the wisdom of feathers and footholds.

In time, I grew simple
and small and the heron looked at me once and did not flee.
I learned to go to the fields and lie down
among the cattails leaning, the goldfinches double-dipping in flight,
my face at rest and washed with sky.

To feel foreign I eat an avocado,

scoop out the seedy gizmo
gut the oily flesh
and spoon it into a bowl.
I lean back, watch the sun's yellow
inch across the tree tops.
Suddenly I am aglow, my lips
shined up, licked with luck
by what once filled the brown husk.
I am like the uninvited
ambling through a desert town,
a stranger who barks and drools
and humbles herself, while dwarfed
by sky and dirt.
I am swallowed, memorized.
There is no holy wanderer.
Look, a hand,
which is a warm cup of failure, fingers
thinning into wilderness.
Discard the outer body.
Let me be. Perfectly fed and small.

Calling T. From the Cultural Wasteland

I'm here in the fields where the crows are many and large.
In the present I am inarticulate.
In the tall grass I can look up and feel adrift.

I'm a slow sinner,
sleepy and swarming with both brides and bridegrooms.

I'm akin to the one hyacinth in the bed, malformed and too few-petalled,
a crooked blue; think of an angel, both scalped and crowned,
its heartbeat spilling into the furred soil.

Some days, I am plum skin. So much holed up in a songless mouth.
I know my place. When you say waste, it's like a sigh continuing.

My teachers: the kinglet's scarlet sore, so open, like the tulip
that taught me one color; a swab of wind; the fetus, like many moments
                                                        rivering.
So sure I failed them.

The mind tires, but the perfection of instinct is like the sparrow's crown
                                                        of white.
Alone in a field, digging out from the self,
no need to usher me to the light. I prefer the slack and aimless willows.

In this field of silence there is a world of coats unbuttoned,
tails blowing behind the crowds of knowing and of not knowing.

I wouldn't care if the hummingbird, the plainer, shadowed one,
drilled its beak into my throat and left it there.

I will take you to the desert

thrust my fingers
into the crease of your thighs
& shack you up
with lantern light.
I'll be slumming you
all the way down.
Buckle scars & skies
so black & glorified,
I'll invade, skirt you dry, swat you,
whittle, spin your crank.
I'll deck you out in yellow grace,
fade out, rename us
painted ground, sand in the teeth,
blooming rabbit brush
standing in for sun.
Jabber on you fancy thing.
Hard-wired for lips, the jaw,
the zealot's drive, I'll roll with you
in bits of basin bones,
wash you in this dusty fire,
& hash you out.
Crested wheatgrass
tangled around my wrists,
soon you'll be dabbling in my salty arts.

THREE.

Marriage

I dunk one slice of cucumber in rice vinegar
and eat—feel the cold tart dissolve.

An afternoon spent
talking ourselves into our own separations,
until the flash of a flicker's shadow on bark.

—ɯ—

In the scat were spoonfuls of broken bones,
a tiny rodent skull.

—ɯ—

All morning I played with the scrub jays
at the edge of stillness,
coaxing the stun of their blue-bright bodies
through the open glass door
with nine peanuts lined up.
I sat in the chair, learning the whip
and dash of bird required for proximity,
learning my own statuesque delight.

—ɯ—

In the back alley, three sparrows dipped
the whole of their bodies
into water puddled in a landscape of dust.

Then on Lander Street, a pothole, two robins,
wetting down the spread-edged feathers,
nearly flowering in the mud of it.

—m—

The river makes real the dreams of lingering,
dead thistle and the blood-willed eye of a towhee,
snow that breaks the fall of snow;

inside the warbler's mouth—a human pink;

to find love late, a string of hosannas;

waiting on a storm, a wild sleep
settling in;   no more seeking,

no more tearing after wind or woodflute—

only shapely dark and warbling.

—m—

I blew a barrage of water gnats down
the rock as I sat at the edge of the Truckee;
like pepper flakes they descended, rode
the hard slope of my breath to the river
on this cold March, Sunday afternoon.

—⁓—

Some days at the refuge—nothing new.
The usual gray coots
without the bright-headed contrast of their young,
a slew of squabbling geese, a mallard or two

beneath the crayon blue sky.
Even now, only the jumbled buzz
of a blackbird alight on some far off reed.

—⁓—

Prayers for even the quickest glance
of a bobcat or one fox's scraggly tail.
Oh Lord, for a pronghorn.
To stare one in the eye. Crazed with longing.

—⁓—

And plainness, oh plainness,
how fine I am with you,
the pinion jay feather I find
along the Carson, its blue sadness
so stunning at once I blaze and weep.
This is what it is like to be joined,
walking the river, a feather in hand,
mounds of dirt that rise above,
a quiet near distorted, undeserved.

FOUR.

I love what comes; I love what goes.

The startle of ice,
a cloistered barn of small town fear,

Spanish lavender that thrives,
sunken rabbit tracks gone hard in snow,

neighbor light, elsewhere,
backyard grief,

the posture of a cold wren,
fir needles that when broken smell of tangerine,

the itch of chickadee claws on skin,
fluency & daughtering,

sanctity of pin, of edge, of neat prayers,

the insanity of wheat.

To Ruthie Harper, the Girl from Third Grade
who Comes to Me in Dreams

You've rambled in my head all these years,
your round face and wiry hair, my guilt
caught up in those blond strands. You walked to school
bragging on the Holy Ghost who bit your neck
while you danced for Him in a church I'd never see,
a church tucked back in woods out on Jakin Road.
"No," my daddy said, "Those roads out there
are tangles in the dark." You cried for me,
swore I'd burn in worthless fields.
I'd call the girls to steal your barbie dolls
in tattered clothes, their crayon-marked arms
hollow, their hair rugged as your own.
We'd rip them from your hands,
tearing limb from plastic limb before we buried them,
marking their graves with stones. Still you smiled.
We didn't understand the scriptures you sang out,
as we dug for the deeper dirt of our burial ground.

Your face seems almost pretty looking back.
In dreams sometimes you come to me, walking
fields of brown, wearing that paisley dress
hanging loose as skin behind the arm
of an old woman who is always there.
She turns the soil, pulling out lemon rinds,
a patent leather shoe with a buckle
and a strap, the kind your mama made you wear
when you were much too old.
We mocked your mama and her broken teeth.
Still there was always your defense, your smile,
the sound of verses on your tongue, drifting

down to calm me after all these years.
In my dream I'm walking into your mouth.
It's soft. I'm sitting down and suddenly
I'm sleeping there inside your complicated grace.

On Starlings

How seriously can I take these speckled scoundrels
that bicker on a branch all morning long?
It's with a kind of jubilee they scrap and scour

for their share. Though I can't help but feel affinity
for the fussy bills that hound their own breed,
yesterday I sat in judgment of the squawks

that raged as if the pleasure of this world is argument.
Ill-willed, they're nothing like the junco—the darling
at my feeder now, a nervous joy who wears,

unknowingly, a tiny mustache made of snow.
Long ago I heard starlings were the ugly birds,
and so stood shocked to see the gleam of them,

smoothed down and touched with flecks of temple fire.
Should I turn from their beauty too frantic and difficult
to believe? No, I'll take the crabby hearts in hand,

let them have their ungodly temperaments—
tree tempests, dazzlers, knuckle-headed saints.

The birds are making me

day by day, building me
with twigs and flecked notes
mistaken for song.

When you realize you've not
once touched your maker,
each act of progress is a mantra
and a trauma. The bird
is not a symbol, but a live thing
with breath so spare
it can't be sucked toward the human;
still I pretend we share the smallest doses
of quiet and disbelief.

The birds, wired-up in living,
can go still as stones,
then cascade through their share of sky,
and light unashamedly in cottonwoods.
They create their reasons,
perfect hosts with no need
to walk on water.

At last they've pieced together
my hand into one image alight
with desperation and gratitude.
Yet, I'm alone in my making,
each bird an impetus,
another distant thing, a reason
to pluck the larkspur and pull it near.

Hold

Not one glance of your blue-strung eyes
in this new century; though in dreams you've come.
In last night's sleep you smiled on my new life
as I woke clutching one coarse strand of jubilee.
We dwell in different deserts now,
and I've been taken in, reconfigured, held.
The birds have flung themselves against my face
and lived. My husband fills in the window cracks
and wraps the pipes. Right now he's out in 20 degrees
bleeding brakes, so proud of his nimble fingers,
small like yours, that can reach into a motor's hidden nooks.
I've not changed much, though I've seen coyotes,
learned the names of birds and desert plants.

Long ago I walked into your story, one I didn't know.
Now, I see the way you braced against it
to make it hold; one dirge you found in everything,
the river lily, lipstick, the Cornish hen that burnt,
forks you bent and left beneath your kneeling bench.
Your story is a troubled hive. I thought I had to live there,
but it never held, and yet I've tucked a shred or two
into my sleep where you appear to reprimand or praise.
I want to say it is my story now, a wink of sky,
the sun that rises, yellowing us all, the birds
quivering with grief—my imaginary hold, not yours.
The desert light is furious; we learn to live with it,
and then we start to crave its sting, forget the trees.
It's not that you're a figment, but rather I'm a thief.
I pocketed your story; I'll weave your memory.

Washoe Lake Bird Refuge: Three Days

I.

The sweet-faced snipe hunkers
in a fringe of grass before it stands to walk
the marsh's edge, sparring the ground
on those stammering legs.
Its body the color of grass; the long bill
maneuvered like a wooden tool,
and everything blending dully into nothing,
then out again. Earlier I dreamed conception,
and it stuck—that gush of wonder
when you stare into the earth and find
such a strange beast prodding the wet.

II.

Shedding their chunkiness,
today the subtle snipes quicken,
leaping over one another
like overgrown hummingbirds in a stir.
Three unspool, airy and delicate, from the mud.
In their liveliness lies disbelief. And inside my body
I feel syllables of light unthickening,
pentecostal songs and notions of fluttering.

III.

After the miscarriage, I return to the refuge
without grief, yet the torque of nongrief unbearable.
Disorder in the sky—snipes displaying
with their hollow songs, low and quavering.
Males, in a bravado-plunge, as if summoned
with the force that only yesterday left my body.

I want to reach up and clip them as they whirl
groundward, to own their descent,
until my face, uptipped and failed, unlocks,
delights in their urgent raga, their ritual of chorus, union,
two dangers on fire in this treeless valley.

A Familiar Chickadee Spotted while Hiking
on Vacation in Montana

And suddenly you were there, little chickadee,
mixed in with the stink of sage
and chirping out our homesong,
the streaked notes, the familiar Ozark-drench
entering this underworld of plentitude.
The pain of it all gone belly-up
as you plucked every hymn out all at once,
the finest silver threads,
pores plumb-full with the rush of light,
our one body, a spasm in God's grass.

No Explanation

I wish there were something of the world I could explain today,
like the way my father used to scratch circles on a stone
inside a box to call a turkey, how he'd practice hours, failing
to match his handmade yelping to that of a bird he never saw.

Or better yet, how my neighbor with the broken body weaves,
her white hair flat against her head, the brown patches of scalp
showing through. If only I could name each small part of her loom,
describe the tools gleaming in blue hands, make good use

of words like weft and warp, then build a phrase for the way
her fingertips will trail beyond her last slow days of work.
But the world's so far away I can't get to the fire of landscape,
the birds minding their own lives, the wild urge of a day spent rambling

blindly past the coyote's blur. I want to kneel again, walk the woods
and scoop the earth's honey, take a breath strung into a thread of amber.
Instead, I'm making do with sleep, and an old brown dog on the doorstep,
his eyes the almost-green of a dirty sea.

Tomatoes

On Jim's side of the duplex, tomato plants rise
from their bed, naked and damp in their strange smell.
It is November, and their fruits are still so full
of themselves, still deepening,
rounding out, wobbling in the wind,
doing what tomatoes do before the rip and tear.
Jim can't get out of his bed most days,
but he listens from his darkened room,
and knows there is no rain.
His hair greasy against his head,
he crawls into the light and hoses down the earth
where the tomatoes have found themselves
basking in their own flames.
If I catch him at it, he'll say to have my pick of them.
He invites anyone who passes to take some,
the men delivering my furniture,
the gray-haired chef next door who just got out of jail.
Jim says he likes imagining their future of sweetness,
but that seems to be all he likes.
Today before he shuts the door,
he says there are riots in France
where boys set a crippled woman on fire
and left her in the streets to burn.
At four the mailwoman, delivering the bills
and glossy ads, stops at Jim's early girls and lemon boys,
plucks one and bites down. On good days
he waits for the stir of her outside his window.
On bad ones, he sleeps the sun away,
but only after delivering the water
and shuffling back to the dim and sour bed,

the tomatoes left to their own power,
their curves, clean, justified.

After Illness

Some days I say the world's a polluted stream of last breaths,
but a day of walking is like passing through a mountain, breathing
                                        air that tastes of pears,
watching the crow's beak shine like sunlight on water,
one shape calm and glistening in the sky.

Give me the trees, slick with green, their pocked wood and sleepy roots.

I want the grass, the quick rain, the pangs from stones in shoes,
                        the slowness of feet worn harder than their years.

Give me faith in the plain twigs, bone-thin horses in a field,
                        a turkey vulture parked in the deadest tree,
                        the distant thought of pole beans steaming in a pot,
the orange daylight
        of a hundred butterfly weeds blooming on a hill.

A long walk leaves this mouth quiet
                        as weathered cedar limbs on moss,
as honey locust thorns lurking in the brush.

Would I give up walking for a room of golden coins?
Or still these soles into stiff shadows
for bellies full of rice, or perfect bodies bowing naked at the feet?

Yes, I've come back to the crook in the heron's neck.
        In flight it pulls its legs along like forgotten walking sticks.

Standing beneath a thousand blackbirds headed home,
        a wash of wings

storms across my face.
Each step invents companion roads, drowsy dreams of pines,

a slew of hungers, satisfied and turned for home,
      sinking in
            and sleeping in the worn brown chair.

Blackberry

Dew-licked,
teetering & ripe,

crypts plumped up
with bright drizzle,

this purple-witted seed-star,
earth-lodged & lonesome,

old prophet once pleasure-shy,
now aching in thornlight,

sway, roothold, desire
whipped fast with impulse,

hands reaching, rippling, riddling—all
to bring the old sweet trinket home.

The Bird Watcher

Again he's out at dawn, wasting himself in a shroud of morning,
wide-eyed and wandering fields of switchgrass

in wading boots. In pale gray light, he slips among their waking
only to return to a stronger light,

after walking out three miles, then back in a morning flooded
                                        with the fervor
of the mockingbird, one know-it-all crow

forcing its loud stories into air, the scissor-tailed flycatcher
hovering above the chicory

unfolding its blue fist, one man lost to the open world.
He's found his element, bound to fields,

eyes flitting over skies and treetops, his skin ruined by
                                      the red-veined heat
of sun—the warming air, his primary belief.

Perhaps he names the birds, *Mercy, Chatter, Demon Fire.*
His love for them is a mansion with no rooms,

no walls, no windows, no iron door. Tilting back his head,
                                      he sees the way
they work above in vastness, where they can roam.

Eckhart says the nobler the powers are, the greater their ability to detach—
the ordinary meadowlark breaking out

across the fields, its yellow belly—worlds away from fingertips—darting
above the stir of grass. I want to pause

for its faithless wings drawn away, then inward, and for the man
who believes he feels the instrument of flight

beating within his sacramental feet.

Rain

Like a dark miracle, they sleep, 2 a.m.
at a truckstop outside Indianapolis;
my husband of three cities, three years—
flycatcher, scrub jay, kingfisher;
our baby daughter, little chickadee,
pale wrinkle, my inkling.
A motherless girl who now mothers,
I am loved twice, two orchids, two glimpses
of the afterlife, two clearwing butterflies,
two fox sightings—twice scraped, twice owned.
A cold rain splatters into neon
and the random chill of trucklight
while my husband breathes slowly,
as he does everything, his lips full and parted.
We are a family of flight, tracing the hunger
of this country, half ravished and heading home
to Georgia as the world calls us to sleep.
Staring at my husband's hands of clarity,
skin smoother than mine, I am trespassing
into a field of orphan lilies brushed with sun,
am given two smooth stones, crushed by a blessing.
I have forgotten my sister, the dark-eyed junco.
There's only night and rain, husband, babe, sleep,
this black string of small good things.
We are not young parents, but this moment
contains a visible trace of newness, shielded
like my daughter's eyes, though shut,
alight with the color of sky and earth.
Praise her intent awakening. Praise her sleep.
Praise the rain's joyful tapping—again, again for grace.

Crocheting

At first in twitches too quick for hope,
her slender needle flits

into the soft-looped sigh of yarn,
lifts off as if a bird jarred awake—

that hot-ironed evangelist of flight
who whips her feather robes and flees.

Bearing the sharp gleam of the needle's craft,
she serves its touch, the needle

leaning in, pulsing like the living do,
and she becomes a simple slip,

a twist, an even breath. Her blood-lines
sweetening to attention, she remembers why

her needle came: for no more than the pattern
of its yarn-trail sauntering

into the piney root of sleep, while the ghost of it
wakes into a thousand rings of fire.

At last, she finds the plainest way and makes
one stitch; one stitch; one concentrated stitch.

Silenced

Never mind the beetle in my mouth, it's gentle.
Never mind this morning, the first sighting
of a lazuli bunting on a branch. I tracked back
to the canyon three days so I might set eyes
on the maker of the song and name it.
I stood there hushed before its blue-laced dip and swift
unsettling into brush, clean blue-white delight,
the tiny neck marked by red nearly that of my home dirt.
Never mind this quiet scoured by sun. I've been muted
more than once by lesser things: fashion, cleverness
peppering its tricks, fugue, scrim and rivulets of mind,
brilliant cross and savviness. Savagely alone, today I am
voluptuous with bird and air, plain-witted prayer,
Sierra canyon shade, unheard and never mind.

Washoe Lake Bird Refuge Revisited

Today the birds provide no solace,
the ibis standing lock-kneed,
looking off disinterested,
the night heron barking as it flees,
one marsh wren so jittery it blurs full-time.
Days like this, my every prayer's half-here,

my hard-fruited presence gone too soft,
its edges spoiled by fog and hours.
Wandering all moss and stupor, I dream
the fence posts damp, drum up finches
making hymns from sky and threads of air.
Then I spot a coyote moving in the sedge.

We catch eyes; he stops short, turns,
sprints across the field, stops, looks back,
then he's off again until he parts
the distant grass, drops back to a prance
that is so purely wild and light
I feel my every hair ablaze and lifting,

the world now tight-grained,
like silk rippling with sun. I've been claimed,
woken up, taken back again.
The August hills skinned
beneath the plumlight of this sky,
the birds reborn and everywhere,
their songs strung tight around the breath.

American White Pelican Colony

Bear River Migratory Refuge

They come wearing old man faces,
bright and washed with sea
or something like disaster.
They float on the water's tension,
their necks elegant, lined with wet fringe,
flat eyes, unflinching in the glare of noon.
The nearest glows like a white-haired monk,
quietly devoted, after he's given up
contemplation, unsung his vows.
The sky, stripped to blue, is clear.
Nothing ghostly, nor vague.
Strong shoulders open to a spread
of wings revealing black tips,
the swash, rise, the reptilian flight.
Pelicans everywhere, like answers
to failed questions. No pangs. At ease.
They dip fiery purses to water,
scratch their backs with the tip of flame.

Rapture in the Ouachitas

Suddenly the whole world is answer,
the trees becoming you, their green music
smeared across your face like the calling of honey
and you glow a green fire beneath a sky
that now wears the girlish darting of your eyes.
Clearly you've wandered into the woodsmoke.
Perhaps the tree bark opens and drips
the blue union of skylight, the wind busy
tampering with the edges of the black gum.
Perhaps at the center of disintegration the blood
becomes *that secret blind love pressing,*
and it all joins in on one shakedown, one rising,
one merging into wren, deer tick, creek noise—
everything one breath dying across the good land.

Advent

The world races for the light,
the priest said before she sang.
It's time to go into the dark, slip into our ugliness.
Oh lover, when she sang, she wore your face.
Her head dropped back, and I was lost in a heat

that took me from the self into the night.
For God, she opened her robe, calling up
her own dark stain. It was not God
I yearned for, but for her, to have her wash
my feet and touch my skin.

Oh lover, hear me out: I want it all,
the spare twig glazed in ice, the garnets slipping
from my hand to yours, the tongue of God,
the dark grief of trees, the dance of hips,
the empty bowl, the grace

of devils, saints, every guilty branch.
I'll ram myself into wholeness,
then shred this body into every unheard
prayer, and then we'll build an earth that thrives
and hungers for the rain's complexity,

a rain that makes us churn and pant while running
for each damaged corner of the night.
Oh lover, did you see her head fall back,
her eyes slipping under?
Open me up and give me that.

First Sighting of the Belted Kingfisher

Little swelter of the wet
      plunge, you leave me daft
            and trembling in your featherwash,

until even the pond water is worthy of ecstasy.
      Virgin to your flair, I've gone giddy,
            fluttering into a joy that thrives at the lip

of vanishing. Sweet drug of presence,
      spry little droll, oblique oboe,
            how do you bear this exuberance?

All along you were in me, voiceless and empty,
      until across the fingers of water,
            you made yourself known.

Woman of whispers and omens.
      Empress of impermanence. We are here.
Now. Full-up and singing.

Acknowledgments

Grateful acknowledgement to the publications in which some of the
poems in this collection first appeared, sometimes in slightly different
forms or with different titles:

Arts & Letters: "No Explanation"; *Ascent*: "The Wolf"; *Atlanta Review*:
"The Back Walkover," "Rainstorm"; *Bellingham Review*: "The Preparation";
Calyx: "Washoe Lake Bird Refuge: Three Days"; *Cimarron Review*: "The
Bird Watcher," "Blackberry"; *Cincinnati Review*: "American White Pelican
Colony"; *Connecticut Review*: "Departure in New Mexico"; *Crab Orchard
Review*: "To Ruthie Harper, the Girl from Third Grade who Comes to Me
in Dreams," "Up in the Cottonwood"; *Flint Hills Review*: "Spiderwort After
Storm"; *Green Mountains Review*: "After Illness," "Sabbath," " First Sighting
of the Belted Kingfisher"; *Image*: "Rain"; *Kalliope*: "How My Mother
Died," "Perfect"; *Massachusetts Review*: "For good,"; *Midwest Quarterly*:
"Once"; *National Poetry Review*: "On Starlings," "Calling T. From the
Cultural Wasteland"; *New Orleans Review*: "Motherless'"; *Quarterly West*:
"Tomatoes"; *Shenandoah*: "Crocheting"; *South Dakota Review*: "Marriage,"
"I will take you to the desert."; *Southern Review*: "Touch"; *Sou'wester*:
"I love what comes; I love what goes"; *Terrain*: "Silenced"; *Third Coast*:
"Carolina Chickadees," "Washoe Lake Bird Refuge Revisited"; *The William
& Mary Review*: "To My Mother's Death."

"Prayer" first appeared on the website of the yoga magazine, *ascent.*

"On Starlings" and "Calling T. From the Cultural Wasteland" appeared on
Verse Daily.

The italicized excerpt in the poem "Rapture in the Ouachitas" (p. 67) is
taken from *The Clouds of Unknowing and Other Works* (Penguin, 1961)
author unknown, translated by Clifton Wolters.

I would like to thank The Nevada Arts Council, The Sierra Arts
Foundation, and The Walton Family Foundation for fellowships and
grants that supported the writing of this book.

I would also like to thank Memye Curtis Tucker, Sandy Longhorn,
Tony Tost, Adam Clay, Shaun Griffin, Mike Walls, Davis McCombs,
Michael Heffernan, Gabriel Fried, and Russell Avery. Special thanks
to Doris Gordon.

And most of all, deepest gratitude to Bill Notter.

ABOUT THE LEXI RUDNITSKY POETRY PRIZE

The Lexi Rudnitsky Poetry Prize is a collaboration between Persea Books and The Lexi Rudnitsky Poetry Project. It sponsors the annual publication of a poetry collection by an American woman poet who has yet to publish a full-length book of poems.

Lexi Rudnitsky (1972-2005) grew up outside of Boston. She studied at Brown University and Columbia University, where she wrote poetry and cultivated a profound relationship with a lineage of women poets that extends from Muriel Rukeyser to Heather McHugh. Her own poems exhibit both a playful love of language and a fierce conscience. Her writing appeared in *The Antioch Review, Columbia: A Journal of Literature and Art, The Nation, The New Yorker, The Paris Review, Pequod,* and *The Western Humanities Review.* In 2004, she won the Milton Kessler Memorial Prize for Poetry from *Harpur Palate.* She is the author of a book of poems, *A Doorless Knocking into Night* (Mid-List Press, 2006).

Lexi died suddenly in 2005, just months after the birth of her first child and the acceptance for publication of *A Doorless Knocking into Night.* The Lexi Rudnitsky Poetry Prize was founded to memorialize her and to promote the type of poet and poetry in which she so spiritedly believed.

WINNERS OF THE LEXI RUDNITSKY POETRY PRIZE:

2008   Tara Bray, *Mistaken for Song*
2007   Anne Shaw, *Undertow*
2006   Alena Hairston, *The Logan Topographies*